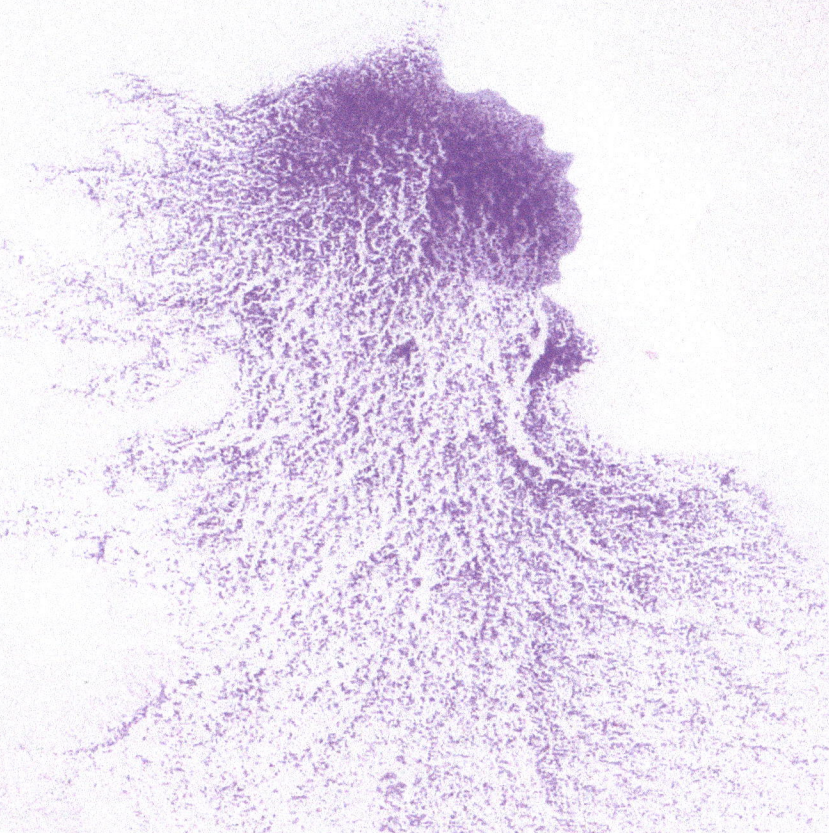

soft *whispers*...

small *shouts*...

deep *waters*...

RUTH HAMMOND

First published in 2014

Free Reign Publishing
103A Harris Road
East Tamaki
Auckland
New Zealand
www.freereignpublishers.co.nz

© Free Reign Publishing
© Ruth Hammond

www.softwhispersbook.co.nz

IBSN 978-0-473-46232-1 PBK
IBSN 978-0-473-29927-9 HCR
IBSN **978-0-473-46180-5** EPUB

Design and production——The Zoo Ltd.
Editing by Sue Beguely——Triplecoil Script.
International listing Ingram Spark 2018——uploaded by Wild Side Publishing,
www.wildsidepublishing.com

All rights reserved.

This book may not be copied, reproduced or transferred by any means whatsoever without the written consent of Ruth Hammond.

Please direct any queries to Ruth Hammond:
hello@softwhispersbook.com

DEDICATED TO
those who seek soft whispers,
small shouts and deep waters...

RUTH HAMMOND

it all began...

One midwinter night, I found a new mystery gently interrupting my sleep.

Three times I thought I heard my name softly being called. Gradually I surfaced. Was I imagining that voice? There was both a familiarity and a difference about it. Bed was so warm. I snuggled lower down under the covers. Suddenly alert, heart racing, yet fearfully reluctant to investigate the sound from the night, I listened intently.
Silence. Nothing but silence.

A quiet, persistent thought repeatedly invaded my mind.
'I want you to get up and write.'
I tossed and turned. Fear left. A new awareness linking heart and mind evoked a silent conversation from within my being.
'Lord, you don't really mean it … do you?'
It was 3.30 a.m. on a cold winter's morning and I seldom woke in the middle of the night. Yet, ever so gently I was being disturbed with this repeated thought, 'I want you to get up and write.'
Bed was so comfortable, a warm haven from the cold morning air. Stubbornly, I snuggled lower. The thought persisted, and persisted. Sleep would not return. New words came into my mind. Somehow I had to capture them. Resigned, I slipped quietly from between the bedclothes, blindly felt for my
dressing gown, fumbled for my glasses and crept downstairs.

The night was silent.

With pen and paper gathered, I began to write. Words came tumbling into my mind, followed by blank spaces.
I waited. More words. Silence. And then even more words were followed by silence as if the silence was waiting for me to get the words on paper. It was as though a stream of knowledge had been sifted, sorted, untangled and presented with a crystal clarity.
Pictures flew through the screen of my awareness.
Capture them! Capture them! Capture them with word pictures telling a truth containing all these shades of understanding. A fancy-free imagery with a central essence to be caught.

Suddenly it was complete. I knew it. This piece had come to an end, and like a tendril winding itself throughout the experience, the knowledge came as to who this was for. Would I have the courage to pass it on? What a task!

Obedience. Obedience to this small voice? This whisper was so delicate it carried with it the choice to hear or not to hear. Timidity. Was this really happening, or was it a figment of my imagination? Trust. Life-changing miracles had come from trusting this whisper before. Faith. Step out believing. Could I bring myself to step out?

Well, it is twenty-eight years since that night. Did I deliver the writing to the person I thought it was meant to be for? Yes, I did. Somehow, it connected at a level that amazed me.

And the writings kept coming.

Words flew into my mind. Pictures filled my imagination, insights into the depths of emotional hurts that people were carrying entered the core of my being. I checked the writings with my spiritual mentor before even daring to share them with anyone. How could I presume to share messages that were not like my usual pragmatic thinking? I was absolutely bemused by it all. And yet people were encouraged and refreshed by the insights the words conveyed.

In response to the first writing, as well as many more over the next three years, one person's reactions truly amazed me: my husband's.

Can you imagine how I felt as I broke into the usual morning ritual of Weetbix and toast at the breakfast table to say, 'Something strange happened to me last night. I felt as though I was stirred from the depths of my sleep to get up and write. I'm feeling really weird about all this, but I think I'd like you to read what I felt led to put on paper.' I handed him my hastily written words. My breathing constricted and my eyes anxiously scanned his face as I awaited a rejection of something so foreign to anything I had ever shared with him before. I experienced a vulnerability of my soul and yet I was wanting to be totally open about this strange experience. His first quick glance gave way to closer attention. He slowly placed the half-eaten slice of toast onto his plate and silently read to the end. And then his tears flowed. The writing had touched his emotions.

Over the next months the writings continued. He became very protective of them, dated them and photocopied them. I was far more casual. If a piece got lost then I believed it had landed where it was meant to go. This casualness was not for him. He treasured the writings and was strengthened by them.

Three years after the first writing my precious husband died from cancer. Months after he died, I put my pen aside and carefully stored the collection of over sixty writings in a folder. I treated them as treasured mementoes of a gift that had brought a depth of peace to troubled times which had turned our lives upside down.

A few years ago I felt challenged to publish the writings. Through a chance meeting, I was led to share my original writings with a new friend who was concerned because she was experiencing a similar motivation to write as I had. Guess what one of the messages was that she had received? Yes, I was to reopen my folder and free my writings. Amazing! Did I listen? Did I obey? I listened, but didn't follow through with publishing. Self-doubt won and I threw away the keys to releasing a gift of hope and encouragement for others.

What did it take to relinquish those keys and free these words?

My experience has been that within the ordinary things of everday life, extraordinary things can be recognised when listening for God's guidance.

As always, it is in the desert times of our lives, when we least expect anything good to happen that miracles occur. A day came when my younger son died without warning. I had gone to his home to pick him up and take him out to lunch. Instead, I discovered that death had claimed him. I believe it was as much a surprise for him as it was for me. For me, a desert time had crashed into my life uninvited. I was unprepared for it and found it as invasive as the eruption of Vesuvius must have been for the inhabitants of Pompeii.

AND THE MIRACLE?

*It was an absolutely unexpected feeling of peace and an inner strength that I would have believed impossible to experience at a time like that. It upheld me through all the important decisions that needed to be made in such circumstances.
I discovered I calmly switched into coping mode: calling police, telling family, making a statement, contacting friends, organising a funeral, writing and delivering a eulogy, receiving messages and flowers and food and visitors, clearing his flat and having it blessed in readiness for the next tenant, donating clothes, food and furniture for those in need, writing letters of thanks, and, finally, undertaking the last, earthly ministry of love, the burial of his precious ashes.*

I was given strength to support family and friends through all of this. I was astounded, for in the midst of the sadness that I carried was this amazing peace. For me this was a miracle from God for which I give thanks daily.

Then, one day, words came into my mind again as they had all those years ago. The depth of the love for my son emerged from my soul to form a new writing. I decided it was time to reread the collection. To my utter amazement I found many of them speaking directly to me. They brought a comfort and an even deeper peace. Suddenly I knew that the time had come to free what I had received. God had been patient long enough and in spite of my slowness to obey had blessed me beyond anything I could ever have believed possible.

*The time had come to ignore timidity,
        to obey him,
               to trust him,
                      and to step out in faith.*

Contents

	PG.
... for as in all deserts the Word travels in the air to be breathed ...	14
...'tis a costly journey, this journey for truth ...	16
... come near to me ...	17
... give heed to my voice ...	18
... your spirit to mine is entwined ...	19
... of nothing else are You worthy ...	20
... seek me, I am here, precious one ...	21
... the everyday things new beauty brings ...	22
... step through the shadowed glass bringing nothing ...	23
... the vision is free ...	24
... grace is the thanksgiving ...	25
... the wings of your song soar to places unknown ...	26
... disturb not such seeds as love, faith and hope ...	27
... the sonic booms in your life can be stilled ...	28
... my love for you flows free ...	29
... softly, softly, as gentle as mist ...	30
... the pendulum's swing an eternity brings ...	31
... a praise and joy unending ...	32
... purest notes of lasting joy ...	33
... from one side of eternity to the other ...	34
... I am ever with you ...	35
... as the wings of time expand and soar ...	36
... in communion unto eternity ...	37
... your sight is now opened to life's overview ...	38
... my word is a channel of grace ...	39
... for each and every one of my petals is free ...	40
... for I have made it so ...	41
... my compassion sees into the heart ...	42
... and so it is in the everyday things ...	43
... it is hope returned to humankind ...	44

	PG.
... forgiveness and love are gifts that are free ...	45
... we travel on a path untrod ...	46
... help us to see more clearly ...	47
... it brings a chance redemptive glance ...	48
... a soft glimmering on the sands of time ...	49
... your presence will bring a fragrance ...	50
... in the moments of such nearness to agony ...	52
... the dark of the night can often bring fear ...	53
... spread forth your wings ...	54
... the gift you can give ...	55
... in everyday life we each can him bring ...	56
... the judgement's not ours ...	58
... the love I can give you has measure unknown ...	59
... new hope to the hopeless ...	60
... to experience new life ...	61
... the most gentle whisper ...	62
... practise my presence ...	63
... no space is too great and no moment is too small ...	64
... to give yourself to me ...	65
... a chord is struck, a choice is given ...	66
... to acknowledge the things we can't see ...	67
... a loving tryst which he empowers ...	69
... which gives guidance with love ...	70
... you are in me and I am in you ...	71
... so much you have seen, so much you have heard ...	72
... the ear must hear the message given ...	73
...we travel on a path untrod...	74
... for I have made it so ...	75
... so come to me, as if a child, and nestle in my arms ...	76
... my comfort will be your strength ...	77
... to believe in such love an difficult be ...	78
... let go of the fears which tug at your heart ...	80
... it is not for all to see the furrows that you tread ...	81
... my love enfolds and embraces you ...	82
... for me you live ... and others too ...	83
... so travel with God in the warmth of his grace ...	84

... for as in all deserts the Word travels in the air to be breathed ...

Come to me, precious ones.
    My heart delights in your diversity;
    my crown is made of you, my precious jewels.

My jewels are in need of further cutting and polishing.
    Are you really seeking me — or the desires of your intellectual imagery?

You fear sharing my freedom
My kingdom can never come under earthly power
    How tightly are you going to hold onto me?
    For I am a free spirit — not in this box or that,
    but a flowing spirit of purity and truth
    not to be bound or confined by my church
    but to be cleansing and freely available.

In a way my church is like a well — the well
    where I met the woman who needed my forgiveness.
Without a gathering point for my water,
    how can people find me?

My well needs a solid foundation of prayer
    (the saints have prepared it before you).
The holding stones do not need to be perfect:
    chipped, scarred, moss-covered, not one perfect brick.
In your eyes a building of insignificance,
    so easily despised for all its imperfection;
    you could stumble upon it — kick it and say,
'I want nothing to do with this imperfect structure which covers my Lord.'

'I am not smothered by it!'

Its tatty structure covers a foundation beyond your dreams,
    for I, the Living Waters, are clean and bubbling,
    pure and refreshing for those who come to my well
        prepared to drop their cup deeply for refreshment from this spring.

Do not worry about the structure of my watering hole
    for, as in all deserts, the Word travels in the air to be breathed.

How long can you live in the desert without coming to a well?
    True, I have many wells built by different engineers;
    wells ground by the sands of time.
    Do not be put off by their seemingly crumbling structure.
    You don't have to worry about the material of the framework,
    I have looked after that for centuries.

This underground stream flows upon a bedrock of granite
    of a type you have never seen.
    My bricks are of this rock;
    they have not been smoothly mass-produced,
    but are infinitely precious because of their chips and dents.

How I love the bruised and fallen — for in their imperfection
    they can embrace one another and become a wall of strength.
This imperfect, humble edifice is not to be despised.
Choose your well and make known its existence
    for I need every chalice I can get at each of my watering holes.
You are wandering in the desert, going from waterhole to waterhole,
    looking for the most perfect structure as an edifice worthy of me.

I am the Lord of humble dwellings — who uses the imperfect
    in order to better display my perfection.
    If I did not, and used a perfect building,
    the building would be worshipped
    and I would be hidden behind the glory.
Forget the structure!
    In bumping into it, people open their eyes and see me.

Look at me. Listen to me.
You can show the way to me just by looking at me,
    for the sincerity of your glance upon me
    and your steadfast following of my Spirit in obedience
    is of the new structure which can be found only in the old.

Heed my word,
    for I too had to choose an old well
    with a structure of decadence on a foundation of rules and regulation.

... 'tis a costly journey,

this journey for truth ...

Faithful to me you're called to be
    from the depth of your innermost being.
Through a desert you've crawled,
    With steadfast eyes seeking a well,
    a deep well harbouring the deepest spring
    of fresh, clear, bubbling water, which gives life and growth
    to the reason for being from here to eternity.

It is a costly journey, this journey for truth
    for the opportunity to grow
        into a dimension of freedom which is mine alone.

Drink deeply.
Your refreshment will be a blessing to others.

... come near to me ...

I am the Lord of gentleness.
Come near to me as a baby deer in the forest
    searches for a spring of clear, pure water.

I desire your obedience — forgiveness of others —
    a purification process worthy of me.

Listen to me, for I the Lord have spoken.

... give heed to my voice ...

Sing to me a new song, everyone:
   a song for which there is no end,
   a praise worthy of the Lord your God.

Joy will be your anointing at the end of the age —
   Come to me all who who are brokenhearted,
   the burdens you carry are not yours alone,
   I am there with you through thick and thin.

Listen to my voice — it is long since I have spoken:
   reassure my people of my love for them.
   A new dimension I bring to them — it is a gift
   for all time — a path of redemption — a renewal
   of spirit — a journey unending.

Thanks be to God.

...your spirit to mine is entwined...

This is a journey unending
    of love and laughter and friends;
    freedom gained by none other
    I bring you a new song.

Come unto me, my precious one,
    I hear at a depth that is unheard.
    my ears are fine-tuned to none other,
    for in your pain I am moved.

Sing unto me a new song,
    a song of acceptance and joy.
    The time for grieving is over,
    your heart I wish to employ.

Come unto me as a lover
    whispers quiet the depth of the soul.
    For other than me there is none
    who offers peace for the soul.

Your spirit to mine is entwined
    like the stems and the stalk of the vine.
The life-blood I give you is ever
    mingled with mine over time.
To come to my throne I am longing,
    a humbling and bending of knee.

Do my word...
    Trust my name...
        Prisoner of none, you are free.

... of nothing else
are You worthy ...

This song of praise is unending,
    it flows as the river of life
        comes tumbling, twisting and turning,
    rushing, a strong, mighty flood.

Of nothing less are you worthy;
    a timeless, ongoing stream
        of voices and praises unending,
    a song to be sung by a few.

My creation of you has been many;
    the sands of the desert are thus.
But you are my chosen — my glorious
    a harmony of song throughout time.

So sing me a new song, my precious.
    I know your struggle of old;
        it has been the struggle of many.
        Don't pass by — but come into my fold.

... seek me, I am here, precious one ...

You, my child, are a thing of beauty
    a jewel beyond measure of value.
The fragrance your petals enfold
    is open to be shared with many.

Come to me, child of mine
    unburden your soul to Me.
    I have carried your burdens
    before the winds of time.
Seek me; I am here, precious one.
    for your fragrance is a balm
    for the sick and suffering.

Your tenacity is a gift not to be mocked;
    there is a great need for you among my people.
Come to me, be refreshed by me.
    Be joyful, for with me the baggage is light,
    the new contents beautiful
    and the journey beyond compare.

... the everyday things new beauty brings ...

Child of mine, you are of light divine
    a vessel of incomprehensible beauty.
Your flight to me of necessity
    frees you to eternity.
These words of mine rejoice for all time
    for I have been with you through the pain and the grime
    and now you are free as a bird in a tree
    with a vision of me to steady thee.

See how I soar; life's not a chore.
    Your view of the world has uncluttered;
    the everyday things new beauty brings.
A temple for me — you're gloriously free.
    Keep it holy and pure, for when you're unsure,
    mixed-up and confused, feeling abused,
    step out as of choice, hear the peace of my voice.
As the eagle has soared with a vision adored
    your chalice from me shared with new clarity
    is a freedom divine that only I give.
    So rejoice and unto me, live.

... step through the shadowed glass bringing nothing ...

Freed in the sprinkling of the water of my blood
    a creature of new time you have come unto me.
This earthly life of yours is a journey in which
    your search for me is the prime priority.

Do it now! Don't put me off as a chore
    to be cast aside for another day.
    There is an urgency in your seeking me
    that speaks of longing and desire to find the reason for life.
Unclutter me of rules and regulations; love of me is not a duty,
    but a freedom in joy gladly given.
Step through the shadowed glass bringing nothing
    with you but your desire of me.
There is work to be done in preparation for this journey:
    the price of your ticket is repentance for your abandonment of me.

Forgive!
    Forgive others for all the pains you have taken into yourself;
    so many of them are of your perception and not their intention.

Confess!
    The time and space that has come between us, you and I,
    produced by the fetters of your mind, have clouded the purity of me.

Receive baptism!
    Water and my Holy Spirit,
    an outward sign and an inward grace.

I do not promise you an easy life, padded and pain free,
    but a new dimension I bring you — a new way of seeing things —
    an awareness of me in all that surrounds you.

So enter this life of richness and joy, peace and security
    with the confidence that only I can give you.
    Journey towards me.

... the vision is free ...

This task that you carry is not yours alone
    but a song of redemption for me.
The vision is free, a new eternity
    which carries commitment for you unto the mists of unknowing.

This commitment you share to the task and the vision
    is to be for each other and to me.
To pass it on needs a mirror of the foundation
    from whence it comes;
    your love for one another is to be as for me.
The knowledge you share is beyond compare of many
    who walk my way.
The path you will tread will be slow and weary
    when measured by human eyes alone.
But underneath this, a personal bliss
    for the forgotten wanderers who search in the rough, stony places
    will have their feet soothed by balm and their souls set free.

A reflection of me is what you're to be.
How you care for each other sings to your brothers and sisters,
    the pattern is easy to see.
For those you are teaching have eyes of discernment
    for the wind that ruffles the tree.

*... grace is the
thanksgiving ...*

Every morsel that we partake
    is in communion with him
      for he has created everything.
It has flown from himself,

and so, in a sense, we partake of him
    in all that we eat.

Stop! Think!

Grace is the thanksgiving to employ in preparation,
    give thanks for everything you eat.

... the wings of your song
soar to places unknown ...

Clear the way to me:
    the path is free to the mysteries of my spirit.
As you enter the set of life's stage you will see only me,
    a guide to life's highways and byways.
Between us a glance of love, pure chance to be seen
    by others in need of this friend.
To glorify me brings fresh harmony,
    and the wings of your song soar to places unknown.

It's a pleasure unknown, this life of your own
    when you respond to
    'Come unto me.'

... disturb not such seeds as love, faith and hope ...

Deep is your trust for me, child of mine.
    You are the treasure for whom I died so willingly;
    your faith has set you free from much which
    still clutters the eyes of many.
The purity of your glance upon me
    brings the promise of new truth to many
    of your brothers and sisters who search
    for a new depth to life which is rooted
    in a soil ripe for germination.

So many are the avenues down which you have come,
    clearing the weeds and the undergrowth
    of the experiences of your life.
Each root of separation from me you have wrenched without mercy
    in your effort to discover my desire for you.
A gardener you are in this field called 'life'
    and many precious plants I have left
    for your discovery in my purpose.
A weed can sometimes a seed of life's truth cover.
Disturb not such seeds as love, faith and hope
    but water them knowing that tender, daily care
    will bring blossoms of delight to share.

... the sonic booms in your life can be stilled ...

Eyes only for me can set you free;
    tune into the depths of my compassion.
The wavelength to me is supremely important —
    for the clarity of my message can be distorted by static.
Home in on my messages,
    unscramble them and read them afresh.
The flutterings of distraction can reduce my word
    to the whisper of unnecessary murmuring,
    a sound to be brushed off in a moment of fear.

Yet my word is that which will set you free
    from the sounds of much clamouring.
The sonic booms in your life can be stilled
    by knowing my still, small voice.
Keep me close, precious pearl of price unknown
    in the treasures of my kingdom.
I long for your obedience, in this journey of unknowing,
    during the moments when time stands still.

... my love for you flows free ...

Oh, how I love you, Saviour of mine
 to the depths of my soul unmeasured.
My love for you flows free to be spread
 to your glory
on the winds of time throughout eternity.

... softly, softly,

as gentle as mist ...

Healing is a mystery from realms unknown,
    God's Spirit free to whisper to each of us
    in ways we do not know.

A touch here, a glance there, or an uplifting
    of indescribable joy.
Physical, spiritual, emotional, mental
    all linked with each other.
How are we to know the gifts we have been given
    until we unwrap them.

Softly, softly, as gentle as mist is the healing power
    which surrounds you.
The fragrance of my Spirit permeates the whole
    of your being.

Gently, gently, I enter the inner courts of your memory.
    A new broom of featherweight wispiness I use
    for the deepest hurts and aches.

Open the windows of your mind,
    allow the gentlest of dustings to become the richest source
    of cleansing you have ever known.

... the pendulum's swing an eternity brings ...

Swinging into the sands of time like a pendulum
    of a clock ticking slowly
        the mighty tree stands tall and free awaiting
        the wind's whispering touch.
As a leaf on that tree desires to float free into
    the journey of autumn's unknowing,
        so, for you and for me, each step of our life
        can obedience seek
        to the whisper of our loving Creator.

'Come unto me, you who are tired and weary,'
    the words of comfort are saying.
We kneel and sigh with an emptying cry as
    the burdens of life, linked with his sacrifice,
    tumble free as dead, withered leaves.
The breath of forgiveness releases sins webbed —
    ill-gained flotsam —
    that frees us to be unto him.

Uncluttered and free, God's new time we see with eyes
    unfettered by hour hands,
    the pendulum's swing an eternity brings of being with him.

Free from internal strife, the journey of life
    with new vision soars,
    uplifted by currents unseen:
    'My Lord and my God',
    is the song we should offer
    of praise that's unending,
    a timeless ongoing stream.

... a praise and joy unending ...

Pure and free let my thoughts be
   as I daily awake unto you.
May my moments of worship become
   a lifestyle of prayer,
   a praise and joy unending.

... purest notes of lasting joy ...

Songs of praise without ending,
    words of joy ascending.
Hear the words we offer thee,
    timeless in supremacy.
This with love our hearts outpour
    an endless knocking at your door.
Saviour, it's a heartfelt plea
    in love we want to honour thee.

You, our strength in hours of need,
    in our praise we are agreed.
From our deepest souls employ
    purest notes of lasting joy.
    Sweeter, higher, let us bring
    eternal notes, our offering
    of daily praise with you we share
    in thanks for your eternal care.

As we rejoice with heart and soul
    the echoes round this earth unfold
    to others in their hour of need,
    your precious Name in glory's freed.
Saviour help us at all times
    to sound the purest of your chimes
    of harmony in love for all
    for whom the plea of justice calls.

... from one side of eternity to the other ...

This song of praise unending brings you close to me.
Share it, share it wider, wider, and louder, louder
    for as the sound swells, as the wave on the shore
    echoes with a tumultuous roar,
    so the sounds of timeless praises shall reverberate
    from one side of eternity to the other, with a seamless
    join   which shall go on and on.

It is your praise I seek. In your world of hustle and bustle
    you are inclined to forget me.
Recall me to your presence always; carry me with you
    in the deepest, quietest place of your being;
    invite me into the place that only I can fill,
    for I long to communicate with you
    in the hurly-burly of your everyday things.

There is nowhere I cannot go and nowhere I have not seen.
    But to the depth of your innermost being
    I will not enter uninvited,
    for that is the place prepared for me alone,
    which empty shall remain until that moment
    in time you open the door to me.

... I am ever with you ...

Fill the hungry with good things: the sound of my Name,
    the joy of my promise of forgiveness to all who seek me.
    For I am the God of forgiveness and love
    whose mercy has a depth unending.

This longing for me cries out, unrecognised
    throughout the whole of your society.
People have forgotten how important I am
    to their total well-being.

It is not fashionable to acknowledge me.
Forget fashion! Seek truth!
    I will give you the courage.

Proclaim my Name and all that you know
    about me and my ways
    to those who on the surface of their lives
    are not even aware they need me.

To moments of aloneness I call you:
    aloneness from the world
    but not from my presence.

I am ever with you to strengthen and guide you.
Don't be afraid; obey only me.

... as the wings of time expand and soar ...

As the wings of time expand and soar
    into and through eternity,
    so, my God, does your boundless love
    regenerate throughout time.

For within all your creation is built
    the capacity to recreate;
    and thus it flows not only through nature
    but also through love and compassion.
    For forgiveness and love is the nurturing ground
    for further forgiveness and love.

How I praise you and give you thanks for this creativity
    which is of timeless procreation.
The earth and the heavens shall reverberate for ever
    with your praise.

... in communion unto eternity ...

*Fellowship, that sweet communion you have with me
    and with one another,
that precious relationship which I enter
    at a depth unknown.
Fellowship is within Trinity — just as you are
    with each other and with me.
    Come unto me in fellowship,
    in communion unto eternity.*

*It's the unknown I wish you to accept
    with me beside you.*

... *your sight is now opened to life's overview ...*

Disturbed by warnings that are not few
    your sight is now opened to life's overview.
Fear not! I too by Satan was troubled.
    Somehow when I'm close his energy's doubled.
The answer's the same for you as for me:
    keep your eyes fixed on God to eternity.
    Stay close, read my Word, pray continually.

The cross was my journey to cover you.
    The cost of my life was a price above earth;
    it had to be so — it brought your new birth.
    The horror of Calvary before time was set;
    so others and you could not forget
    the love of your God was given for all.

Turmoil, unrest, division is spread;
    doubt, indecision, outpourings of dread.
These are the ways of the devil, my friend;
    your mind and your feelings, do not towards them tread.
Assurance, love, grace are gifts only from me;
    the price has been paid for others and thee.

The sins of the world will always disturb,
    the weaver of them can never be free.
    Tricks of deception are what he can bring,
    so open your eyes and unto me cling.
    It's obedience to me on the journey you seek;
    your protection's assured: I died for the weak.

... my word is a channel of grace ...

This world of turmoil and confusion is around
    all of humankind.
My word is a channel of grace to be shared with all
    those whom you meet.
Do not fear what can follow my word in order to test it,
    or destroy the good it brings.
If those who had gone before you had stopped,
    because of what they feared would follow,
    then my word would never have reached
    those who needed it.

Remember the sower, and the ground upon which his seed fell.
The truth of that parable endures for all time.

So take courage my friends: the Word is about to be sown in
    your land in a mighty way.
Much will fall upon good ground;
    just as much will fall on stony ground.
You need to share the 'Good News', and to care
    for those who come to your well.
Let there be no division between your wells,
    but an acceptance of each other
    that recognises dependence upon the underground stream
    which is your source: me.

... for each and every one of my petals is free ...

Free as blossoms' petals in a summer breeze
    you are basking in my love,
        for I have loved you from before all time.
Awaiting you has been fulfilled by your gentleness
    and appreciation of my creation.
        Enjoy it, my precious one, for few have eyes
    to appreciate nature at such depth.

I long for you to know me at a depth
    you cannot imagine.
I too knew hurt of soul through misinterpretation
    and inaccuracy of perception.
The freedom from rules which I came to give
    has been sorted into boxes and prisons
    of various kinds.

But I am beyond that. No longer am I
    a victim of others' expectations.
Neither are you:
        for each and every one of my petals is free
        to be in the currents of life.

My journey was hard, but it bought your freedom.
Relax and enjoy my creation and journey towards me.

... for I have made it so ...

You, my precious one, are perfect in my sight,
    for I have made it so in the price I paid on Calvary.
The ministry I give you is a special one
    which requires your fine tuning to me.
    You will see what is of me and what is not,
    so pray earnestly to walk in my truth.
Little things will bring my warnings, and through
    your gentleness will be passed on and heard.
The sincerity of your growth in me brings much joy.

    The path you tread is blessed.
    Be not afraid, be not alone,
    for I am with you forever.

... my compassion sees into the heart ...

The truth of my Name is to rightly
    be brought alongside historical prejudice.

My Name has a power all of its own;
it cannot disown freedom, truth and justice.
Beware! Look and see your discretion is free
    from viewpoints of others; look to me.

My compassion sees into the heart.
    Called are you too, to see with new sight;
    listen to others as they uncover their plight
    of misunderstandings through their journeys' twists.
    Their closeness to me is covered in mists
    of duties, expectations and the sights others see.
    They're frightened to share their insights of me.
    Of all expectations and miseries they're free.
    It's a call of obedience only to me,
    for the spot which they stand on
        brings a difference of view
    to the viewpoints of others, refreshing and new.
    So share with each other from all vantage spots;
    conformation of vision will not be your lot.
    Then put them together: a picture you'll see
    made from small jig-saw pieces, an unveiling of me.

... and so it is in the everyday things ...

I share much with you, child of mine, which others
    cannot see,
Judgment of others is mine alone, not man-made trials
    of heresy.
I died for all, that all might live; your faith
    has set you free.
The ups and downs, the ins and outs, is knowledge
    just for me.

The spread of my knowledge and creativity goes further
    than man can ever measure.
    The good which I can create out of evil and destruction
    is mirrored in the resurrection which came out of the crucifixion.

And so it is in the everyday things that
    humankind is left free to choose what
    they will see.
    Some may stop short at points in time,
    an end and judgment made.

The cross at Calvary was such a moment for those
    who followed me.
    But you are called to see past such moments,
    to see the good which I can create out of the bleakest situations,
    to carry hope into all things at all times.

... it is hope returned to humankind ...

The point in time when all stood still
    occurred on Calvary's hill.
When hope was dead for those he'd led
    his suffering seemed for nil.
But God has taught us much, my friend;
    it was not in vain he died.
    Without Good Friday we couldn't heed
    the joy of Eastertide.

For in the depths of great despair,
    a message we can hear:
God suffered too for me and you
    his love forever true.

And thus it is for us to see
    in depths of misery,
Jesus has been where we have trod,
    the journey is not new.
It's hope returned to humankind
    through all he said and did.
His triumph over death brings joy
    that never should be hid.

... forgiveness and love are gifts that are free ...

Consumed by a fire that's burning inside
    hatred can grow like spring's neap tide
    advancing and soaring, a huge crushing wave.

The worm-eaten soul becomes a cavernous cage
    in which misunderstandings bring insights of blight,
    and others' perceptions are judged as of right.

It's dangerous to float on such flotsam in life;
    the rip-tide will toss you in danger and strife.
    Grief, sorrow, bitterness in time can become
    the destroyers of hope when given the rudder.

'Tis relief to share grief when life's torn asunder;
    the compassion of others is a balm steeped in love
    birthing healing and hope to a soul torn apart
    and out of the struggle can come a new start.

Forgiveness and love are gifts that are free
    to those who repent in their journey with me.
    Seek deep to the roots which tear at your heart,
    confess them to me, — it will bring a new start —
    a beginning washed fresh in forgiveness of others,
    a deep sense of cleansing and wholeness which pours
    in a stream never ending.
        Close not the doors.

... we travel on a

path untrod ...

We travel on a path untrod;
    Life is a journey unto God.
Eyes on Jesus at all times,
Holy Spirit be our guide;
never let us leave his side.

...helps us to see more clearly ...

*Father, it is in our own walk with you that you desire of us
     honesty and truth,
a willingness to listen to the breath of your Spirit
     within each and every moment of our lives.
Our glance is not to be deflected to the walk of others,
     other than to receive encouragement to keep our
     eyes centred on you.*

*Nothing escapes your vision, or is too small
     to go unnoticed.
There is nowhere we can hide
     from your eyes of discernment.
For you have a sight which encompasses
the roots of our blindness.*

*Take the scales from our eyes, so we may see
     the reality of our sin,
     those attitudes that mask our vision of truth,
     the truth which you see
     and which we desire to perceive.*

*The stumbling blocks in our journey of relationship
     with you and with others,
     help us to see more clearly such obstacles
     for they hinder us on our journey
     as servants to each other and to you.*

... it brings a chance redemptive glance ...

A little test you showed to me
    to measure how I tread.
It has to do with fellowship
    of resurrected dead.
The test, it seems, is of a type
    that we don't wish to see.
It bares the truth before our eyes
    when journeying to thee.
And yet I'm glad that you have shown
    this measure for my sin;
        it brings a chance redemptive glance
        to errors deep within ...
Of mercy and forgiveness held
    with grievance deftly hidden;
        a self-protective barbed-wire fence
        my own inflicted prison.
Mercy's glance will break this stance
    of others unforgiven.
The test you see, is how would it be
    to welcome them to heaven.

... a soft glimmering on the sands of time ...

A soft glimmering on the sands of time
    this word comes to encourage you that you are mine.
Precious and obedient, listening and yet free
    my word you will carry to eternity.
The pattern you seek has yet to be seen;
    some pieces are missing in ground in between
    now, and the future of a more definite theme.
Patience is hard when you fret to see more:
    the unheard and helpless understand to the core
    of their beings in life's turbulent stream.
    The despair you now bear in agony's drift
    will bring understanding, in fact it's a gift!

For those you will serve will journey the path
    that you are now treading with tedious steps;
    those without justice you'll call to new hope.
My covenant's a promise
    to all,
    for all time.

...your presence will bring a fragrance...

*Blackness and despair are not 'forever' moments in your life,
    but the shadows which give depth to the overall picture
    which is made of many jig-saw pieces.
These shadows, painful as they are, have a hidden depth
    which cover a priceless gift.
        For it is in the bleakness, the dry and arid desert places
        that I am to be found.*

*I hear your call; I even hear the heartfelt whispers
    which have not been thought, let alone uttered.
I know your despair: the numbness, the lack of colour
    which pervades the inmost depth of your being.
And yet, like the deepest well in the driest desert, in your
    depth of being, you will find me
Just as the freshest, clearest water runs hidden in an
    underground stream.*

*For in finding me, you will discover my love for you.
    I too have been where you are now treading;
    forty days and forty nights I trod in the desert alone
    Seeking the 'I am' of 'I am'.
It was not easy: Doubts and temptations troubled me
    along the way;
    and yet that desert experience became my strength,
    my rich resource for all I had to face.*

It was a gift for others; my compassion has an
                everlasting truth for all time,
My suffering has been a balm for others.
Your suffering will be a gift to others you will meet and
    in my service you too will understand their pain.
And your presence will bring a fragrance in the midst
    of their bleakness and despair.

Your healing is assured.
    Bring your pain to me in moments of distress,
        but look around too for the things you can give thanks for,
            however tiny or minute,
    for I delight in your praise and thanks.
You have a perception of the beauty of my creation
    and I enjoy sharing it with you.
I am the Way, the Truth and the Life and, strange
        as it may seem
    you are journeying to me.

... in the moments of such nearness to agony ...

Temptation — a tension between choices—
'I too had temptations.'
In the wilderness many temptations came before me;
I knew the 'I was ... I am ... and I will be,' that is, the totality of 'I am'.
I knew I could use my power: it was, is and always shall be.
The temptation was to use my power indiscriminately
    for my own superficial, earthly needs of the moment.
I knew what I had to face before my earthly life was over:
    there were two moments which I knew would happen
    and yet I pondered.
I knew, but I hoped I would not be tempted beyond my endurance
    when in the middle of them.
For to have the power I have must always be for good and never for evil.
    I have decreed it so.
The 'taking on' of humanity brought with it the weakness of all humankind
    and there was a tension between power and weakness.

And the two moments?
First, the garden of Gethsemane. I had known of this moment for all time.
    In the moment of such closeness to agony,
    sadly, I knew I would ask the Father to take this cup from me,
    yet I also knew I would walk in his will.
    It was that moment of choice which had the power
    to bring doubt with it.
The second moment was in despair:
'My God, My God, why have you forsaken Me?'
A moment of anguish voiced — pulled from within me — and yet I knew,
    I knew that God had not forsaken me.
There was a tension in the desert between knowing I would say it,
    but hoping I would not.
Temptation: a tension between choices.

... the dark of the night can often bring fear ...

Sweet sounds come to a musical ear,
    but the dark of the night can often bring fear.
An openness of heart to all you receive:
    the ups and the downs, the highs and the lows
    eternally swing in life's ebb and flow.

But peace, perfect peace at the depth of the soul
    is what I can offer; you will remain whole.
    For in giving yourself, in turn you'll receive
    more than your reasoning will ever believe,
    a small step in faith will steady the soul.

You can't see or touch music, it's free in the air.
    It's the same with my word, it's eternally there.

... spread forth your wings ...

You each have the choice to say yes,
    or say no as you listen to my voice;
    such an ocean of freedom has been yours
    from the beginning of time.

In the depth of your being is a place that's far seeing;
    it can tune into your will or mine.
The message I bring to eternity does sing
    the truth can ne'er be ignored:
    It's 'Come unto me — O precious be free,
    fly where the eagle has soared.
    Spread forth your wings
    as air currents swing you
    to places and venues unknown.'

The turbulent air — not seen is still there —
    a fact universally known.
The sureness of me, invisible to see
    has yet by many to be heard.
The burden's not yours to open the doors;
    it comes with the power of my word.

... the gift you can give ...

Come unto me all who starve to be free,
    your quest is for waters of life;
    a free-flowing stream of mercies unseen
    is as near to your soul as your dream.

Step into life!

Don't hide behind strife of questions and answers unseen;
    your reason can't prove the depth of my love,
    Its mercy is of measureless mien.
The gift you can give, is unto me live,
    an outpouring of heart, soul and mind.
The anomaly's thus:
    you receive your gift plus,
    a life that's eternally free.
For the joys and the depths, the worst and the best,
    will be lived through in communion with me.

... in everyday life we each can him bring ...

Good news travels fast, as on wings in the air.
    It uplifts the soul from depression and cares
    of the world which from turmoil will never be free,
    yet the burden's not yours; it has been dealt with by me.

Tired and despondent, weak and confused
    is what we become listening only to views
    spread commercially world-wide as noteworthy news.
It seems there's no choice in what we receive
    like smouldering offal drawn from issues which grieve
    the weak and the helpless. They have no reprieve
    from the cold judging eyes which hungrily seek
    to experience depths of misery, then hastily retreat.
'I'm glad that's not me,' we think with a sigh
    and swiftly forget. It's called a 'blind eye'.

The struggle's not ours; the work has been done
    the sins of the world redeemed by the Son.
In everyday life we each can him bring
    to our friends and our contacts and let them discover
    the peace and the joy which can come from no other.
    The choice is all ours to pass this news on,
    an obedience to share the victory that's won.
    Gloom and despair would wither and fade,
    the news of the world could widen its scope
    with a daily review bringing vision and hope.

The choices are ours. God's news is not fashion,
    but to those in deep misery it carries compassion
    an encompassing grace in a measureless ration
    of love without ending. There's none needs defending
    in God's realm of justice, for mercy's unending.

Do we pass this news on, we who've received,
    or mumble and stutter, 'They'd never believe'?
A measureless courage from a measureless grace
    is what we can call on for sharing the faith
    with those he's preparing the news to receive.

A new wave is surging in this day and age.
    It calls us to witness to the One who can save
    those who are teetering on a chasm-like brink
    of the depths of destruction. Their self-worth has no link
    with their Creator who's waiting for them to receive
    good news of Jesus from your lips and mine.

To sweep the shore freely as in spring's high neap tide
    for those who are waiting are as grains of the sand,
    a numberless number which he understands.

Good news travels fast, as on wings in the air;
    you carry the Word within you to share
    with those whom you touch on an everyday basis.
    In the deserts of life, his word's an oasis.

... the judgement's not ours ...

'I do not judge as man judges; I look at the heart,
    and so it has been, right from the start.'

We can never assess motivation or spirit
    of what is behind an action of merit.
It's the same with destruction or acts which seem evil,
    the judgment's not ours. We'd do well to inherit
    wisdom passed on before us, and take it to heart.
    It could free us from error and creating new sin
    for our reaction or action to what we perceive
    may oppose the intention of that which was given.
Our power to misread is one which can grieve
    not only the people who on this earth dwell,
    but the Lord of us all, as we create our own hell.

And so it is thus in the everyday life
    that we can reduce the friction of strife
    which flows from reaction to misread intention —
    suspicious defence is a human invention
    prepared to destruct for a message perceived;
    for we'd rather destroy than give and let live.

Oh, when will we hear the message God sent us
    which showed us in action a call to repentance.
    Our forgiveness received, from within us should action
    ongoing forgiveness, not withholding a fraction
    from those who aggress us or press for reaction.

Strange as it seems, the message is love:
    it unwinds rejection and brings a new start.
We're unable to judge; only God sees the heart.

... the love I can give you

has measure unknown ...

'This is my Son with whom I am well pleased.'
The whisper's as soft as a cool summer's breeze.
The love I can give you has measure unknown,
    it enfolds as a mist wherever you go,
        as you step out in trust your healing's assured
        a zing and a zest will show you are cured
        and free from a mooring strewn with flotsam, a mire
        which imprisons and snares the well of desire
        for joy and fulfillment and peace of the soul.

Look around and about. Your vision has cleared;
    new insights are yours, new sounds you will hear.
    Gently, yet surely new meaning you'll see,
    life is a symphony conducted by me.

Tune in to my word and list to my voice:
    pure water is there, to drink is your choice.
    Untangled from moorings, in life you're now free,
    come with the current and swim towards me.

... new hope to the hopeless ...

Assured of God's love is what we're to be:
    encouraged, uplifted, eternally free
    from misery, corruption and guilt-ridden fear
    of rejection, reprisal and society's bent
    to punish, denounce, outcast and reject.

The spark which for mercy and acceptance could glow
    if embers of hope were breathed on to flow
    into flickers of flame giving birth to a fire
    of a love that's like God's, pure in desire
    for the well-being of all who on this earth dwell.

The message in essence is a cry to be just:
    when we're forgiven, we each then can trust
    one another's new start. Forgiveness and love
    form paths of direction in which we can give
    new hope to the hopeless, a fresh start to live.

... to experience new life ...

Freedom has come from hearing the Word.
    The joy is all ours; life's not absurd:
    There's meaning and depth, colour and flow
    in a spirit-filled life. We just need to know
    of God's love and God's mercy, his quick listening ear.

To walk in obedience carries no fear,
    yet we struggle and toss in life's ongoing stream
    overlooking the fact we are part of his scheme.

To let go of ourselves as we understand
    secures us by faith in the palm of his hand
    to experience new life, the mystery of which
    unfolds itself daily, its tune has new pitch.

We need to hear often the truth from our teachers,
    to encourage our sharing with those who are seekers
    that life's not a burden, it has new dimension.
    The 'chances' which happen too frequent to mention
    are not purely chance when we walk in his Spirit,
    but messages sent, in experience writ,
    which override logic and concepts of fashion.

This journey of ours in the mists of unknowing
    disperses the clouds while to God we are growing.
The glimpses we catch of his overall plan
    bring marvel and wonder at the width of the span
    of his hand in creation of all that exists.

This prayer which is life does not need man-made visas;
    it is open to all who receive and trust Jesus.

... the most gentle whisper ...

Come, Almighty,
    to deliver the pains and afflictions of my dear sister.
    Love and envelop her in the mists of your healing power;
    guide and steady her, always ready to respond to
    the most gentle whisper in the depths of her soul.
Her way has been long and weary; lost and lonely she has felt,
    worldly comfort has no meaning,
    deep is the chasm filled by a tumultuous roar
    which has no direction or vision of light.
But you O Father, you have the power to bring hope
    to those who have lost all hope.
    Father, I ask You to rekindle hope,
    a hope which gives light to a new walk
    a new walk in your spiritual journey;
    a new vision of your wondrous glory,
    a new sense of your eternal presence
    a new vitality in the wonder of you.

My heart's desire is to ask this of you:
    Jesus, I ask you to plead this prayer before
    your Father and mine. In you do I trust.

        Amen

... practise my presence ...

The love I have for you flows from the beginning of time.
> It was there when I created Wisdom.

Before the earth was formed I knew you,
> and I have been with you through the pain and the grime.
> Even when you thought I wasn't there, I was.
> Release to me the depths of your deepest hurts
> for when you suffered, I suffered with you.

In coming to earth I too felt what it was like to be alone,
> apart, misunderstood.
> I hear your plea. So come unto me.
> For though you travail and are heavy laden,
> I will refresh you, and give you the peace you long to hear.

Practise my presence:
> You can carry me in the depths of your inner being.
> I bring serenity with my Holy Presence.

Be free in the breath of my Holy Spirit,
> as free to move in that breath as the thistledown
> when released to the whim of the summer's breeze.
> Float in the haze of the days in praise and worship of me,
> for such worship brings light into the darkness of despair
> and has the power to bring my love into the bleakest moment.

How I desire you to love me,
> for I have loved you from before all time.
> So come unto me, my precious one,
> and nestle in the sureness of my love;

It was for you I died.

... no space is too great and

no moment is too small ...

Prayer is a mystical link between you and me;
    it ties us together with knots you can't see.
Sweet communion it brings in which I rejoice
    not pressured by me, yours is the choice
    to open the door to the voice of your heart
    the sharing of you is where you can start.

Your everyday things I'm longing to share,
    Nothing is too small for my notice or care.
For each moment of you is as precious to me
    as the unfolding drama of earth's history.
    No space is too great and no moment too small;
    I long for your voice, I wait for your call.

The life which I give you I'm willing to share;
    just whisper to me, I'm already there.
It's in love I have come from the beginning of time
    to let you all know: I'm yours and you're mine.

... to give yourself to me ...

How prayer works is not for you to know;
> just practise it so you can grow
> in relationship with me, the essence of which is
> sharing yourself and listening to my voice.

My open link to you is through my Holy Spirit;
> to give yourself to me, is the only way to do it.
Release the ties which bind you firm to that which is of earth;
> my spirit comes to those who do; it's often called rebirth.
Once I gave my life for you, so you in turn may live;
> the moment's come to make your choice
> to me your life now give
> and you will find what happens next
> is true to Bible text:
> new life you get with new percepts, a reason to rejoice.

In giving me your life you'll receive my Holy Spirit.
> New sights you'll see, new ways there'll be
> of understanding life.
Your faith will grow and you will know
> The miracle of me.

... a chord is struck, a choice is given ...

There are times when the Lord speaks to the inmost
    depths of our hearts
    with a still, small voice, a precious message to impart.
So great's His love and the freedom of our choice
    that we can affirm or deny the whisper of that voice.
        A chord is struck.
        A choice is given.
And we decide from whence we've heard a note of truth.

... to acknowledge the things we can't see ...

Long and deep is the time of sleep,
    the time before we awaken
    to the depth of God's love and the meaning of life
    a discovery: we've not been forsaken.

Yet to reason we clasp and to knowledge we grasp,
    seeking the reason for living.
    New dimensions in thought become stretched
    and are fraught
    with anomalies defying our logic.

The things which we trust will perish and rust
    if what only we see we believe in.
Confined by our choice, we hear our own voice
    struggling with questions unanswered.

Both the seen and unseen we're created to live with,
    mixed with truths we can't see, hear or touch;
    we know their existence, yet bring forth resistance
    to acknowledge the things we can't see.
Ridiculous this, when within knowledge mists
    we grasp how a seed hides a tree.

Our journey called life can be freed by a trust
    in the love of a living Creator
    whose giving for living is unending.

The misery we cede comes from man's greed
    in desire to own all that's seen.
Yet we've been entrusted to share all in justice
    whatever the faith, race or creed.

continued ...

The doing of it is the difficult bit
    as a world we fall by the wayside.
The problem's so big as for answers we dig
    that we swing to the view of the hopeless.
Yet God's truth is for sure an answering cure
    to the misery which goes on relentless.

The pattern is thus: we start here, with us
    sharing God by thought, word and deed
    with all whom we touch in our day to day living.
At work and at home we each have the power
    to share 'God is with us', like a cool autumn shower
    which quenches the thirst from summer's outburst
    of sun beating down on the earth.

For those whom we reach then can in turn spread
    the news of a God who's alive and not dead.
Our care is in giving new life to the living
    a freedom which only love feeds.

... a loving tryst which he empowers ...

Forgiveness is a gift untold
    of God's great mercy to his fold.
We are his and he is ours
    a loving tryst which he empowers.
Forgiveness asked, forgiveness given:
    the greatest gift to pour from heaven.
If we will tread where he has trod
    and walk with pureness unto God
    then we must to each other bare
    the deepest hurts and trust his care.
For we've been made for one another
    not just self, but sister, brother.
We've a calling in his Name;
    love and service bears no shame.

... which gives guidance with love ...

We each have a choice to hear your voice,
    that tiny whisper for life
    giving guidance with love
    from eternity's storehouse of wisdom.
The measure you give lets us joyfully live
    within boundaries of trust and obedience.

Yet the pressure is great from your wisdom to break
    to walk through this life with intent
    to feed self-desire. Eternity's mire,
    the hell of the soul we invent
    to escape from your voice.

Yet the message you gave
    was to give up the self
    with its whims and desires
    and give life in service to others.
If we give ourselves thus
    we discover the plus:
    a peace and a joy of contentment.
New energy sings of fulfillment which brings
    a reason for freedom of giving.
The self which we sought
    is an inner resource
    which blossoms like flowers in a desert.
    As we hand to your care what always was there
    we receive a new treasure: a self without measure,
    one we can trust and can share.

*... you are in me and
I am in you ...*

You are in me, and I am in you,
    a fact that's eternally true.
For you reflect me as a mirror reflects light
    in an ongoing beam which can travel forever.
I too can travel as light giving warmth to those
    whom I touch with my love.
And just as with prisms and lenses, my light
    can become a rainbow of love through you;
    a light to glow in dark places
        travelling on the dust in the vacuums of empty souls.
There is nowhere I cannot go and nothing I cannot touch
    in the misery of humanity.
You, my children, are to become the lamps
    which carry my light
    wherever you may go.

... so much you have seen,

so much you have heard ...

The path which you walk holds dangers unseen.
The beginning of it so innocent seems, but
    be alert, keep awake and watch where you tread.
    Whose energy flows from that which is dead?

So much you have seen, so much you have heard
    as your journey unfolds its meandering course.
    Be alert, keep awake, from whence is the source?

... the ear must hear the message given ...

My still small voice speaks to the inner heart
    softly, softly, its message to impart.
    The ear must hear the message given;
    My Spirit is your loving haven.
And so it is in the daily walk of life;
    you hear a different tune which quells an inner strife.
In peace you walk; obedience when given
    frees you from the turmoil to which many lives are driven.
Hear my voice.
    Listen and obey.
        Mists of doubt bring anguish,
            Trust is the only way.

... we travel on a path untrod ...

Free as blossoms' petals in a summer breeze
    you are basking in my love,
        for I have loved you from before all time.
Awaiting you has been fulfilled by your gentleness
    and appreciation of my creation.
        Enjoy it, precious one, for few have eyes
        to appreciate nature at such depth.

I long for you to know me at a depth
    you cannot imagine.
I too knew hurt of soul through misinterpretation
    and inaccuracy of perception.
The freedom from rules which I came to give
    has been sorted into boxes and prisons
    of various kinds.

But I am beyond that. No longer am I
    a victim of others' expectations.
Neither are you:
    for each and every one of my petals is free
    to be in the currents of life.

My journey was hard, but it bought your freedom.
Relax and enjoy my creation and journey towards me.

... for I have made it so ...

You, my precious one, are perfect in my sight,
    for I have made it so in the price I paid on Calvary.
The ministry I give you is a special one
    which requires your fine tuning to me.
    You will see what is of me and what is not,
    so pray earnestly to walk in my truth.
Little things will bring my warnings, and through
    your gentleness will be passed on and heard.
The sincerity of your growth in me brings much joy.

    The path you tread is blessed.
    Be not afraid, be not alone,
    for I am with you forever.

... so come to me, as if a child,
and nestle in my arms ...

Gentleness is of your heart, yet sadness lies there too,
    regrets that all your hopes in life weren't filled as dreamt by you.
And yet within there lives a hope that all was not for nought;
    the dips and crests, the hurts and fears, a battle bravely fought
    has brought you far, and close to me, in this your earthly struggle.
I hear your plea, draw near to me, life is not a muddle.

Forgiveness sought, forgiveness given, is where you all must start;
    grief and hurts held deep to self twist and tear the heart.
Yet when they're brought to me in trust, I understand the pain.
    I hear your plea, hand all to me; my life was not in vain.

So come to me, as if a child, and nestle in my arms,
Forgiveness seek, forgiveness give to all with whom you've shared.
And peace, my child, is what you'll get at depth beyond your dreams.
I died for you that you might live more fully in each day.
I hear your plea, so come to me, my love will with you stay.

*... my comfort will
be your strength ...*

Go to my Word for strength and encouragement.
My ways are not the ways of the world, I call you
    to walk in my ways — love, peace, justice —
    freedom from all which ensnares you
    into measuring security in worldly ways.

Relax, let go, trust me, for I am the Lord your God.
    Come unto me, I am your security.
Time I give you to find me.
Love I give you to serve others.
Forgiveness is the key to the world of inner peace
    which can flow from you to many.
Your journey will not be easy, but with me
    you will find comfort and reassurance.
    My comfort will be your strength.

... to believe in such love can difficult be ...

There are times in our lives when we wish to be free
    of a deep cloak of sadness which smothers our 'me'.
All colours are drab and life has no 'zing';
    the pain is an ache, an encompassing thing
    like a shadow of grief it clings to our being
    diffusing the image of all we are seeing.
The place we are in is surrounded by mists
    of doubts of self-worth which stifle our gifts.
    A wall of protection around us we raise;
    a defensive invention from all that which preys
    in the world which surrounds us just waiting to leap
    to the core of our pain which is solid and deep.

This misery's an ache too deep to cut out;
    its whisper is doleful, an echoing shout.
Yet this burden when carried can truly be shed,
    discarded, regarded as that which is dead
    with no place in our life, with no room left for breath,
    its life-clutching claws powerless in death.
    For its grip on our life can slither away
    as surely as light gives birth to new day.

'How can this be?' you mutter and sigh,
    'I feel so wrung out that I can't even cry.'

The mystery is this: your pain has been heard.
God listens in silence, he speaks through his Word.

The message he brings you is one of deep love
    enfolding, encircling as wings of a dove.

So precious are you in the plan of his day
    that he walks with you hourly as you go on your way.
To believe in such love can difficult be
    just breathe it, my friend, you're eternally free.

... let go of the fears

which tug at your heart ...

Open and free as gulls soaring oe'r sea
    is the trust we're to have as we listen to thee.
An opening of self to glide and to soar
    on currents unseen, never far from your shore.

'Leave worries behind and listen to my voice;
    your life is a road on a map of your choice.
To me you hang on as a child at the knee
    faith is the name of your journey with me.
The future is hid from the view of your sight;
    trust and obey. You can steer by my light,
    the light of my Word as you study and read
    will speak to your heart and answer your need
    to choose the right current on which you can soar
    as you wing your way life-wards steady and sure.
Let go of the fears which tug at your heart.
Relax in my arms,
    my love was your start.'

... it is not for all to see the furrows that you tread ...

Come to me, child of my heart.
Sweetness and grace are yours with diversity
    of mind and heart and strength.
It is not for all to see the furrows
    that you tread.
For you are mine and my ways are not easy.
Draw close as one draws close to one's lover
    empty your secrets, hurts, whisper to me
    for I am the one whose strength and wisdom
        keeps the stars in place.
My heart longs to hear your call,
    child of grace.

... my love enfolds

and embraces you ...

I come to comfort you,
    to give you rest, peace and joy.
I am with you always;
    my love enfolds and embraces you
        for you are my precious child, my love of all time.

... for me you live,
and others too ...

To go on is not to leave behind that which has gone before.
Grief and suffering are still at the centre of your core,
    and yet so are joy and hope, new life, rebirth.
Where you go takes what you are and all you've ever been,
    touches here, touches there, on life's unfolding screen.
For me you live, and others too.
Pick up your life anew.

... so travel with God

in the warmth of his grace ...

Sublime was the time we had, you and me,
    with freedom to be as birds in the tree.
The love that we shared was the breath of the soul
    untainted, unmarred, eternally whole.
The ups and the downs did not shatter its power
    it glowed like an ember or lily in flower.

Love does not die, it's eternally pure;
    the strengths of its cords can stretch and endure.
This parting in time that brings its own grief,
    for me is now shadowed, for you is release.
So travel with God in the warmth of his grace
    enfolded in love as eternal as space.

This poem came from the depths of my knowledge and experience of God's love, enabling me to release my younger son into God's eternal care.

finally...

after this...

are there more writings?

Well, yes there are.
There are still times when words come into my mind and I instinctively know they are not to be lost, but captured. I confess I am bemused by the whole process. My joy is that these words can bring the comfort and assurance of God's love for us. In the darkest of our places He is there for us...but only if we allow Him to be. It is when we extend Him a heartfelt invitation to be a part of our innermost being that His loving peace and strength gently diffuses our soul.

With love,

Ruth

www.ingramcontent.com/pod-product-compliance
Lightning Source LLC
Chambersburg PA
CBHW041709290426
44108CB00027B/2908